Ideas of the Modern World

Communism

Nigel Ritchie

HODDER
Wayland
an imprint of Hodder Children's Books

Published in Great Britain in 2000 by Hodder Wayland, a division of Hodder Children's Books.

This book was prepared for Hodder Wayland by Ruth Nason.

Series design: Simon Borrough

The right of Nigel Ritchie to be identified as the author of this work has been asserted by him in accordance with the Copyright, Designs and Patents Act 1988.

A catalogue record for this book is available from the British Library.

ISBN 0 7502 2749 4

Printed in Italy

Hodder Children's Books
A division of Hodder Headline Limited
338 Euston Road, London NW1 3BH

Dedication
For Oliver, who makes all things possible

Acknowledgements
The author and publishers thank the following for permission to reproduce photographs: The Bridgeman Art Library: pages 4 (private collection/Novosti), 7 (private collection/ Barbara Singer), 11 (Musée de la Révolution Française, Vizille, France/Visual Arts Library); Camera Press: pages 6, 8-9, 15, 17, 18, 23, 29, 31, 32, 33b, 34, 35, 39, 41, 43, 44, 49, 51, 52, 53, 56; Popperfoto: pages 1, 12, 19, 21, 22, 25, 26, 33t, 36, 38, 47, 50, 57, 58; Topham Picturepoint: pages 14, 37, 42. The maps were drawn by Carole Binding.

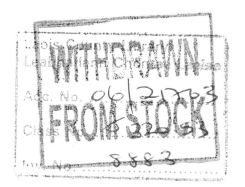

Contents

What is Communism?

Communism came to have a greater impact on the twentieth century than any other political idea. At the height of its influence it dominated the daily lives of over a billion people. Evolving into a universal force for freedom and equality, communism appealed to poor and oppressed peoples throughout the world. It shaped the twentieth century, and will probably cast a shadow over much of the twenty-first.

Since the publication of Karl Marx's and Friedrich Engels' *Communist Manifesto* in 1848, potential revolutionaries have had a dramatic call to arms to which they could respond. From Lenin to Mao, and Stalin to Che, some of the greatest modern figures have carried the flag of Marx's communist dreams across the pages of history. In its most basic form, communism was designed to provide a radical political and economic alternative to the capitalist sytem which permitted the widespread abuses, rising social inequality and appalling working conditions generated by the rapid growth of the Industrial Revolution.

Lenin was the world's first communist leader. It was his version of communism, rather than Marx's theory, which was followed by other communist states in the twentieth century. This painting from 1933 shows Lenin speaking to Red Army soldiers in May 1920.

The theoretical basis of communism

The political and economic writings of Karl Marx (1818-83) were a response to the rapid changes of the Industrial Revolution. They provided an analysis of capitalist society, based on three interlocking parts: 'historical materialism', the division of society into 'base and superstructure', and the 'class struggle'.

Historical materialism

Marx believed that communism would replace capitalism, according to scientific laws of development. His description of those laws borrowed heavily from the German philosopher, Friedrich Hegel (1770-1831), who argued that history was the result of a constant conflict between ideas. Each idea (thesis) created its opposite (antithesis), before the two merged into a union (synthesis), to produce another opposite – and so on. Instead of ideas, Marx put economic

Communism and socialism

The word 'communism' comes from the French *commun*, meaning 'belonging to all'. Originally, communism meant a particular socialist system of society, where property was owned in common and shared out according to need. Socialism meant different things in different countries, but, after *The Communist Manifesto*, communism became directly associated with a more working-class, revolutionary movement. This association was confirmed by the success of the 1917 Russian Revolution, when Lenin founded the world's first communist state.

The modern distinction between communism and socialism can be precisely dated from 1918, after Lenin's successful Russian Social-Democratic Labour Party (Bolshevik) changed its name to the All-Russian Communist Party (Bolshevik). From then on, the international socialist movement split into two camps: **social democrats** (who dominated in western Europe) continued to seek change through parliamentary means, whereas **communists** (who dominated in eastern Europe, Asia, and Africa) rejected the existing political system and sought rapid change through violent revolution.

The Industrial Revolution

Rapid economic development began in Britain half-way through the eighteenth century. The replacement of the traditional agrarian (feudal) economy by an industrial (capitalist) one was achieved through important technical advances, such as the steam engine. As steam-powered machines replaced skilled artisans, factory production swept across Europe, revolutionizing the economic 'base'. From 1830 onwards, the Industrial Revolution spread across Europe and the USA, and on to Japan.

Mill workers in Manchester (1862), where Friedrich Engels' father owned a factory. The new industrial labourers would provide the driving force for change.

production as the driving force behind human development and called his new theory 'historical materialism'.

Base and superstructure

According to Marx, all societies were founded on an economic 'base' divided in two parts: (1) the 'material forces of production' (how people exploit their environment, e.g. by hunting or industry) and (2) the 'relations of production' (how that exploitation is regulated). A social 'superstructure' of ideas, religion, law, and politics was then built onto the economic base to represent the interests of the class that held economic power. Conflict within the base caused changes in the superstructure, leading to a more progressive base.

Capitalism leads to its own downfall

Marx argued that the conflict between capitalism's material forces (factory production) and relations of production (its lack of regulation) created cycles of boom and bust. The workforce that capitalism created soon became its enemy as a result of increasing unemployment and social misery:

'What the bourgeoisie therefore produces above all are its own gravediggers.'

In *The German Ideology* (1846), Marx portrayed the development of human history through five economic bases: primitive communism, slavery, feudalism, capitalism, and (finally) communism.

Class struggle

Marx's view of history was one of permanent class struggle between the haves and have-nots. Historical materialism showed that the capitalist system would eventually collapse, so why should the proletariat (Marx's term for the workers) bother with class struggle? Because history only created the conditions for change. It was men and women who actually made history. However, before the workers could seize power, they had to be politicized and made aware of their historic mission.

What would the new communist state be like?

Revolution was just the first stage. Afterwards, a 'dictatorship of the proletariat' would protect the revolution from its enemies and destroy the existing state machinery (e.g. the police, the civil service, etc). Once communism had been achieved (with the abolition of private ownership and social class), Marx argued that the state would no longer be necessary. Humankind could then develop to its fullest potential.

Communist freedom

Marx was vague about how a communist society would work, describing an ideal communist society

'where nobody has one exclusive sphere of activity, but each can become accomplished in any branch he wishes. Society regulates the general production and thus makes it possible for me to do one thing today and another tomorrow. To hunt in the morning, fish in the afternoon, rear cattle in the evening, criticize after dinner, just as I have a mind, without ever becoming fisherman, herdsman or critic.' (The German Ideology, 1846)

This poster celebrating the third anniversary of the Russian Revolution was entitled 'The Last Decisive Battle'. It shows a typical capitalist being knocked off the world.

Das Kapital (1851–83)

Marx spent the last 30 years of his life on *Das Kapital*, his great unfinished work. It exposed the inner workings of capitalism and showed that the key to its downfall lay in the 'surplus value' of labour.

Under capitalism, the worker works to survive, but the capitalist works to produce profit. He does this by buying the worker's labour-power cheap. Instead of paying the full value (e.g. 11 hours work), he pays only a subsistence value (e.g. 6 hours work). The difference between the two is called the 'surplus value'.

Because profit comes from exploiting labour-power, the rate of profit depends on the number of workers employed. But increasing competition requires the capitalist to expand and buy more machines, and machines have no surplus value, so they cannot produce profit. More machines mean fewer workers and profits fall. Workers are laid off, sales drop as supply outstrips demand, and small firms are taken over by larger firms. These depressions become a regular feature of capitalism and the workforce (which grew with the expansion of industry) eventually revolts against its increasing misery.

The practical basis of communism

In practice, capitalism did not collapse under the weight of its own contradictions, as Marx predicted. Instead, organized labour and collective bargaining led to higher wages and social and political reforms. Revolution did not happen in the developed capitalist countries of western Europe, but in the underdeveloped feudal countries of Russia and China. So Lenin's version (not Marx's vision) of communism became the inspiration for future communist states. By extending the dictatorship of the proletariat indefinitely, Lenin laid the foundations of a modern totalitarian state. This was characterized by a single powerful leader, a highly organized party, and an active secret police. Instead of the state withering away as Marx had foreseen, it grew larger and entangled itself in people's lives.

Communism in Russia and China

Both Russia and China had less to lose and more to gain from communism, than western Europe. The dictatorship that was needed for centralized planning and large-scale development blended easily with Russian (Tsarist) and Chinese (Imperial) traditions of authoritarian rule. The human cost was considered a small price to pay in countries that knew little of Western freedoms. However there were important differences between the two revolutions. Where Russia relied mainly on the proletariat in the cities to support the revolution, China relied mainly on the peasantry in the countryside. Where Russia encouraged large-scale industrial development, China encouraged small-scale rural development. China's example was especially important for other developing countries, for it showed that communism could be adapted to local conditions and did not have to follow the Russian model.

1999: celebrations of the fiftieth anniversary of communism in China. In Tiananmen Square, Beijing, the government displayed its military might.

A new religion

Communism's policy of atheism brought it into conflict with organized religion. The communist state promoted the worship of communist leaders, whose thoughts, images and statues dominated public life. After his death, Lenin's body was preserved for public display, like a religious relic. In China, Mao was elevated to god-like status. Millions of Mao badges were produced and worn; prisoners were expected to bow before Mao's image and confess their sins; and there were daily public recitals of his *Little Red Book*.

A pain-killer, not a cure

Communism's concern with the material conditions of life challenged religious belief, which Marx compared to the pain-killing drug opium. In 1844 he wrote that religion pacified oppressed people by offering (false) paradise in heaven, at the expense of (real) paradise on earth.

'Religion is the sigh of the oppressed creature, the heart of a heartless world and ... the opium of the people.'

Statistics

While communism brought many benefits, there was a high price to pay. Rough figures suggest that communism caused roughly 100 million deaths, from famine, the firing squad, or forced labour: 62 million in the USSR, 35 million in China, two million in Cambodia and North Korea, and around one million each in Africa, Afghanistan, Vietnam, and eastern Europe. These figures clearly illustrate the oppressive nature of communism as a political system.

The gulags (forced labour camps)

Forced labour camps became a prominent feature of many communist regimes, particularly in the USSR, China, and Cambodia. They provided 'political correction' to suspected opponents of the regime, as well as an endless source of free labour. 'Gulag' was an abbreviation of the name of the secret police organization which ran the labour camps in the USSR.

Lenin set up forced labour camps in 1919. At first they held around 100,000 prisoners, but during the 1930s the number escalated to around 5 million per year – the result of Stalin's collectivization, purges and deportations. Millions of prisoners (criminal and political) were housed in camps in remote areas like Siberia, where they were made to work on industrial or construction projects. Conditions were harsh and 15-30 million inmates died in Russia alone.

Background to Communism

The French Revolution (1789-99)

Socialism in Europe emerged from two main events: the Industrial Revolution and the French Revolution. While the Industrial Revolution brought capitalism, the French Revolution challenged the political status quo.

Its doctrine of 'Liberty, Equality, Fraternity' made grand claims on behalf of humankind, but it was never a people's movement. It began as a bourgeois revolt against the unjust rule of the monarchy, nobles and clergy. As the middle classes demanded parliamentary representation, the poorer classes were demanding bread and land. The fall of the Bastille in 1789 symbolized the collapse of the old regime. Then a combination of mob violence, foreign invasion, counter-revolution, and factional struggle brought radicals like Robespierre, Danton and Saint-Just to power. Their attempts to establish a Citizen's Republic of Virtue brought a brief but bloody Reign of Terror (1793-94), before a Directory was established to consolidate the bourgeoisie's new power.

The taking of the Bastille, on 14 July 1789, marked the beginning of the end for the French monarchy.

The rights of man

'Men are born free and equal in their rights ... These rights are liberty, property, security and resistance to oppression.'

By declaring the Rights of Man, and not just of French men, the French Revolution left a legacy to inspire future generations worldwide.

Louis Antoine Saint-Just (1767-94)

Saint-Just was a strong believer in the use of violence as a necessary feature of revolution. He was elected to the National Convention (the French parliament) in 1792, as its youngest member, and immediately made his name with a speech condemning Louis XVI to death – guilty by the very fact of being a king!

In 1793, Saint-Just became head of the Committee for Public Safety (CPS), and a leading figure behind the Reign of Terror. In 1794, he was arrested and guillotined along with his close associate, Robespierre. Saint-Just's ruthless terrorism made a strong impression on the Russian communist leader, Lenin.

Louis Antoine Saint-Just, one of the leaders of the French Revolution.

The use of violence

Power turned Saint-Just into a cold fanatic. His words anticipate the behaviour of totalitarian rulers in the 20th century:

'There are only two kinds of citizens: the good and the bad. The Republic owes the good its protection. To the bad, it owes only death.'

Marx's analysis

Marx characterized the French Revolution as a bourgeois revolution. While it freed the people from the tyranny of king and clergy, it failed to free them from the tyranny of private property. The bourgeoisie, who had grown with the development of capitalism, gained economic and political power. The peasantry gained ownership of their lands. But the poorest got nothing, except the freedom to change their masters. When Marx laid out his own revolutionary tradition half a century later, he made the abolition of the existing property system a precondition for establishing a fairer social order.

The Communist Manifesto, 1848

In 1847, a secret society called the Communist League commissioned Marx and Engels to draw up a party programme. In its 60-odd pages, *The Communist Manifesto* laid out the communist agenda (historical materialism, class conflict, common ownership, etc). Its main aim was to convince workers that change would only happen once they had joined in common cause.

'The workers have nothing to lose but their chains. They have a world to gain. Workers of the world unite!'

History was on their side. This strong sense of destiny gave the *Manifesto* a powerful appeal to revolutionaries across the world.

Revolutionary stirrings in Europe, 1848 and 1871

The opening words of *The Communist Manifesto*, published in 1848, were: 'A spectre is haunting Europe – the spectre of Communism.' However, it was not communism but nationalism that threatened the continent. A wave of popular urban revolts against royal rule rippled across Europe in 1848. Beginning in France, they soon spread to Italy, the Austrian empire, and Germany, where a short-lived parliament was set up in Frankfurt. Most of these revolts were suppressed violently within a few months.

The revolts failed, because they were spontaneous, undisciplined and divided. The moderates who led the uprisings were alarmed at the radical agenda of some of their colleagues and were reluctant to mobilize the workers and peasants on their side. Marx saw the revolts as rehearsals for future revolution and learned a valuable lesson from their failure: the mass of people could not be relied upon to spontaneously support the revolution. First, they must be taught 'socialist consciousness'.

The Manifesto's warning

'The history of all hitherto existing society is the history of class struggles ... Let the ruling classes tremble at a communist revolution.'

The Paris Commune, 1871

The revolt of the Paris Commune in 1871 represented the last gasp of the French revolutionary tradition. In the final stages of the Franco-Prussian war (1870-71), Paris surrendered to Germany after a four-month siege. Outraged Parisians rebelled against the national government and set up their own socialist, municipal self-government, the Paris Commune. It proposed many radical measures. But, before these could take effect, the revolt was bloodily suppressed after a week of ferocious fighting. 20,000 Communards (including women and children) were killed, and another 10,000 deported.

Although the Commune lasted only 73 days, its lesson was long-lasting. Radicals now chose reform rather than revolution as the way forward. And Marx turned the event into a communist legend by (wrongly) describing the Communards' struggle as the first great uprising of the proletariat against the bourgeoisie, leading to the first socialist government. In fact, it was national humiliation, not class struggle, which had

Earlier in the century, Napoleon III had ordered the building of a great column in the Place Vendôme to celebrate his victories. In May 1871, the Communards pulled the column down.

triggered the revolt. However, the French model inspired Russian revolutionaries to form their own self-governing organizations (known as soviets) in 1905 and 1917.

Karl Marx (1818-83)

Karl Marx was a German philosopher and economist. Born in Trier, he studied law and philosophy before becoming a journalist. Expelled from several countries for his radical views, he lived much of his life in exile around Europe. In 1844 he began a lifelong collaboration with Friedrich Engels. In 1847, they joined the Communist League and wrote its party programme, *The Communist Manifesto*.

After the upheavals of 1848, Marx settled with his wife and children in London, where he was plagued by poverty and illness. During this time he produced most of his writings, including *Das Kapital*, and helped to found the First International.

Karl Marx (left), Friedrich Engels, and Marx's three daughters, Eleanor (behind), Laura (left) and Jennie.

Influences on Marx

Marx's ideas were drawn from German philosophy, British political economy and French socialism. But the most important influence on him was his friendship with Friedrich Engels (1820-95), a fellow German. Engels provided financial, as well as intellectual, support, without which much of Marx's later work would never have existed. Engels had left

Prussia in 1842, to work for his father, a rich textile manufacturer, in Manchester, England. Engels' contact with industrial poverty affected him deeply and he wrote up his experiences in *The Conditions of the Working Classes in England* (1844). This work greatly influenced Marx's writings. Together, Marx and Engels tried to steer the proletariat towards their revolutionary destiny.

Changing the world

'The philosophers hitherto have only interpreted the world in various ways; the thing, however, is to change it.' (Marx)

The Internationals

Marx was not just a thinker. He also put his words into action, through involvement in various underground political organizations. The best-known was the International Working Men's Association, which he helped to found in London in 1864. At its height, around 1868, the International claimed 800,000 members (mainly in the UK, France and Germany) and an impressive reputation. With great skill, Marx kept this mixed bunch of radicals, anarchists, trade unionists and nationalists together until 1872, when it broke up after irreconcilable political disagreements. The First International was soon followed by a Second (1889-1919), and the Moscow-backed Third, commonly known as the Comintern (1919-36).

Marx's legacy

During most of his life, hardly anyone had heard of Karl Marx. His name only became associated with revolution after his public support for the Paris Commune. But it was the Russian Revolution which gave him an international profile. Since then, almost every revolutionary movement, from China to Cuba to the Baader-Meinhof Gang, has been influenced by his writings, fulfilling his prophecy that the bourgeoisie would be forced 'to remember my carbuncles as long as they live'.

The Russian Revolution

The origins of the Bolshevik Party

In 1898, Georgy Plekhanov founded Russia's first Marxist party, the Russian Social Democratic Workers' Party (RSDWP). It had a tiny membership compared to its main rival, the Social Revolutionaries (SR), or peasant party. Lenin joined the RSDWP, after he had been imprisoned and exiled for revolutionary activities in the Russian capital, St Petersburg.

Settling in Europe, Lenin worked on the RSDWP newspaper and wrote several books setting out his ideas. He argued that a disciplined party of full-time revolutionaries should be created to educate and lead the masses, and that the peasantry should eventually be included in the 'dictatorship of the proletariat'.

Lenin (left) spent his life building a party to take power, finally triumphing in 1917. Here he sits with Josef Stalin, his successor as Soviet leader.

Lenin's uncompromising views isolated him from other socialist leaders and led to the RSDWP splitting into two at its second congress in 1903. The Bolsheviks ('majority'), led by Lenin, said that revolution needed to be started and led by professional revolutionaries. The Mensheviks ('minority'), led by Martov, said that revolution would happen when the workers were ready for it. Continual in-fighting led Lenin to form a separate Bolshevik Party in 1912.

A revolutionary through and through

A Menshevik opponent described Lenin:

'There is no other man who is absorbed by the revolution twenty-four hours a day, who has no other thoughts but the thought of revolution, and who even when he sleeps, dreams of nothing but revolution.'

1905 Revolution

In February 1905, a mini-revolution in Russia was sparked off by the country's defeat in the Russo-Japanese war and by the massacre of a peaceful demonstration demanding better working conditions. The subsequent unrest, involving strikes and mutinies, led to a general collapse of authority across Russia. Factory committees in the Urals and elsewhere set up the first soviets (self-governing councils) as an alternative form of rule. Revolutionary groups played a major role in events, setting up workers' soviets in the main cities. Returning to Russia from exile, Leon Trotsky became the leading spokesman for the St Petersburg Soviet, which organized a string of strikes against the Tsarist government.

The revolt was eventually crushed and the soviets closed down, though not before Tsar Nicholas II had issued his October Manifesto, which granted agrarian reform (allowing the wealthier peasants to buy their own land) and the creation of a representative parliament, the duma. The duma was supposed to approve all Russian laws, but the Tsar made sure it had no real power, dissolving it twice during his reign.

Leon Trotsky, 1918. Trotsky's most famous contribution to Marxist theory was his policy of 'permanent revolution', which advocated spreading revolution abroad to support revolution at home. This became a key feature of Lenin's thought until 1921.

The 1917 Revolutions

In 1914, Russia joined Britain and France in declaring war on Germany and the Austro-Hungarian Empire. A succession of military defeats, combined with a shortage of food and equipment, caused widespread demoralization. By February 1917, food shortages and a collapsing economy set off bread riots and anti-government demonstrations in Petrograd (the new name for St Petersburg), and the unrest spread rapidly to other cities. Soviets (dominated by Mensheviks and SRs) sprang up around the country to co-ordinate the workers' actions. The growing chaos forced the Tsar to abdicate, and the duma formed a Provisional (bourgeois) Government which ruled alongside the soviets. The soviets controlled vital military orders, as well as basic services.

Bolshevik tactics

From his exile in Switzerland, Lenin sent a telegram to the Bolshevik Party early in 1917:

'Our tactics: absolute mistrust, no support of the new government ... No rapprochement with other parties.'

Lenin, who was still in exile, realized this was the moment he had been waiting for. In April 1917, the German authorities allowed him to return to Russia in a sealed train. The Germans hoped that the Bolsheviks would destabilize Russia and force the country to withdraw from the war. On his arrival in Petrograd, Lenin immediately published a series of demands, known as the 'April Theses', calling for radical opposition to the Provisional Government.

Clever use of 'agitprop' (see page 21) made Lenin and the Bolshevik Party increasingly popular with war-

Supporters of the Bolsheviks at a demonstration outside the Winter Palace in Petrograd, May 1917.

weary workers and soldiers. Lenin's success can be measured by the rapid transformation of the Bolsheviks from a minor party with 20,000 supporters in February, to a major force (dominating the soviets) with 250,000 supporters in October.

In August 1917, Leon Trotsky joined the Bolsheviks. With the arming of the workers (the Red Guard), Lenin was now ready to seize power.

Trotsky's prediction

On 25 October 1917, the day after the fall of the Winter Palace, Trotsky said:

'Either the Russian Revolution will create a revolutionary movement in Europe, or the European powers will crush the Russian Revolution.'

Lenin (Vladimir Ilyich Ulyanov) (1870-1924)

Vladimir Ulyanov was the world's first communist leader. A dedicated revolutionary from an early age, he adopted the pseudonym Lenin to disguise his identity from the police.

From 1900, he lived in exile in Europe, where he founded and ran the Bolshevik Party. Returning to Russia in 1917, he revealed his talents as an organizer and propagandist, transforming the Bolsheviks from a fringe group into the leading revolutionary party. After the October Revolution, he tightened his grip on government by strengthening the role of the Party. With a mixture of ruthlessness and pragmatism, he successfully guided the USSR through civil war and economic reform until his early death.

On the nights of 24-25 October, Red Guards captured key points in the city, before taking the Winter Palace and arresting the Provisional Government. Lenin emerged from hiding to take control, proclaiming, 'We shall now proceed to the construction of the socialist order'. News of the coup spread quickly throughout Russia, and other cities soon followed.

Consolidating power, 1917–18

As chairman of the new Soviet Government, Lenin immediately announced Russia's withdrawal from the war and urged peasants to seize land. As well as dealing with mounting domestic problems, the new regime had to defend itself against counter-revolutionary armies. A secret police force (the Cheka) was formed to control law and order and crush any opposition.

When elections for a new assembly were held in January 1918, the Bolsheviks won less than a quarter of

Agitprop

'Agitprop' is the shortened form for 'Agitatsiya Propaganda', a term coined by Plekhanov and later used for the section of the Communist Party responsible for mass communication (by means of film, radio, posters, and newspapers).

It was Plekhanov's idea to use 'agitation' and 'propaganda' to mobilize public opinion in favour of the Marxist cause. Agitation meant bringing a single idea to the attention of a group. Propaganda meant the dissemination of many ideas to individuals. Agitators used speech and political slogans (e.g. 'All power to the soviets!' and 'Peace, land and bread!') to manipulate an audience's emotions and rouse them into action. They were often the main point of contact between the party and the masses. Propagandists used pamphlets and newspapers to explain complex issues, like unemployment and social injustice.

the seats. The next day, Lenin closed down the assembly, declaring that 'a republic of soviets is a higher form of democratic principle' than an elected bourgeois parliament. Afterwards, the Bolsheviks renamed themselves the Russian Communist Party and moved the capital from Petrograd to Moscow.

By the end of 1917, the Bolsheviks controlled only a small part of Russia. The German army occupied the south, and counter-revolutionary forces controlled the rest. Disappointed at the failure of the revolution to spread to Europe, Russia was forced to sign a punitive peace treaty with Germany at Brest-Litovsk in March 1918. Lenin accepted the treaty (against much protest), as the price to pay for the survival of the new regime.

Wireless stations were set up so that propaganda could be broadcast to workers country-wide. Wireless sets were also sold to peasants at special cheap rates, so that they could listen in to the daily broadcasts from Moscow.

The international impact of the Russian Revolution

The Russian Revolution was supposed to lead to world revolution, but failed to make a lasting impression on the rest of Europe, despite a wave of strikes and civil unrest in 1918-20. Soviet republics were briefly installed in Germany, Slovakia, and Hungary (the longest, at four months). But in these countries, the disintegration of the old order was not as complete as in Russia, and the local communists were poorly prepared to seize power. In Germany, the communists only undermined the post-war government which was already dominated by socialists. The only successful communist revolt happened in 1921 in Mongolia, which set up a People's Republic in 1924.

Rosa Luxemburg (1871-1919)

Rosa Luxemburg personified the ideals of the radical movements that swept Europe at the turn of the twentieth century. A Polish-born German revolutionary and agitator, she played a role in founding the Polish Socialist Party and the German Communist Party (or Spartacus League).

She developed her own interpretation of Marxism, stressing the need for democracy, internationalism, and revolutionary mass action (e.g. industrial strikes). This contradicted Lenin's advocacy of party dictatorship, nationalism and the use of terror. Luxemburg was murdered during the Spartacist rising in Berlin in January 1919.

The meaning of freedom

'Freedom for the supporters of the government ... however numerous they may be – is no freedom at all. Freedom is always and exclusively freedom for the one who thinks differently.' (Rosa Luxemburg)

Civil war, 1918-20

From 1918 to 1920, a terrible civil war between communists ('Reds') and their opponents ('Whites') cost millions of lives and caused widespread destruction. The Whites, led by former Tsarist generals, had no common aim except defeating the Bolsheviks. They were helped by Western forces, who were infuriated by Russia's withdrawal from the First World War and its refusal to repay the Tsar's debts. The well-organized and disciplined Red Army, under the inspired leadership of its founder, Trotsky, fought fiercely for its survival.

Because of the breakdown of the economy, Lenin introduced a policy of 'war communism' to keep the Red Army fed. This meant seizing surplus food from peasants, and made the communists very unpopular. While the civil war lasted, the peasants reluctantly sided with the Reds, as the lesser of two evils. But the defeat of the Whites meant they no longer had to make that choice and they refused to surrender any more grain. Food shortages led to rioting in the towns and countryside during the winter of 1920-21. And in March 1921, the Kronstadt sailors (previously Lenin's strongest supporters) mutinied, denouncing Bolshevik tyranny.

European hostility

The European powers were very hostile towards the new communist regime. Winston Churchill, British Secretary of War, commented in 1919:

'Civilization is being completely extinguished over gigantic areas, while Bolsheviks hop and caper like troops of ferocious baboons.'

In the difficult times after the revolution, these women in Petrograd were reduced to selling their household possessions.

The NEP, 1921-28

War communism may have won the war, but it now threatened to lose the peace. So Lenin introduced the New Economic Policy (NEP) as a temporary measure to regain his grassroots support. It promoted limited private enterprise and allowed the peasants to sell their surplus on the open market. Agricultural production soon recovered. But many communists felt betrayed by this reversion to capitalism and pointed to growing social inequalities, especially among the peasants. Lenin insisted it was a necessary sacrifice – 'two steps forward, one step back'.

The creation of the USSR

In response to mounting criticism, Lenin strengthened his hold on the party by suppressing all opposition. The power of the soviets drained away to the centre, leaving the Communist Party in control of all aspects of life. In 1922, Lenin established the Union of Soviet Socialist Republics (USSR), consisting of Russia (the most powerful), Belarus, Transcaucasia and the Ukraine. Each republic ran its own local matters, while foreign policy and the armed forces were controlled by the central government in Moscow. Contrary to popular belief, the totalitarian character of communist rule was established well before Stalin.

Lenin's succession

Lenin's death in 1924 was followed by a bitter power struggle for the leadership, eventually won by Stalin.

A pun

In 1920, Lenin made this pun on his faith in the power of technology:

'Communism is Soviet power plus the electrification of the whole country.'

Stalin (Joseph Vissarionovich Djugashvili) (1879-1953)

Stalin ('man of steel') was the adopted name of Joseph Djugashvili, who became Soviet leader after Lenin's death. A shrewd political operator, he dragged the USSR into the twentieth century under the slogan 'Socialism in one country'. He pushed through a rapid programme of modernization in industry and agriculture. But high rates of growth came at a heavy human cost. His manipulation of police terror and centralized power created a repressive totalitarian state, responsible for over 40 million deaths. After the war, he added eastern Europe and the Baltic states to the communist empire.

Having played a minor role in the revolution, Stalin became increasingly powerful after his appointment as general secretary of the Communist Party in 1922. It allowed him to fill important positions with his own supporters and gave him a place within the Politburo (the party's ruling body), from where he manipulated policy disagreements to outmanoeuvre first Trotsky (his main rival) and then his former allies. By 1929 he had full control of the party.

The Five-year Plans, 1928–37

Stalin realized that the USSR needed rapid modernization to survive. At stake was communism's boast that it could create a powerful, modern state to rival any created by capitalism. One hundred years of industrial revolution were crammed into two intensive Five-year Plans. Vital heavy industries like coal, iron, steel, oil, electricity and machinery were established. By 1937, the USSR was the second largest industrial power in the world (just behind the USA).

The industrial town of Magnitogorsk was built in 1929-31. This is a view of its Stalin Metallurgical Plant.

The need to keep up

'To slacken the tempo would mean falling behind. And those who fall behind get beaten ... We are 50 to a 100 years behind the advanced countries. We must catch up this distance in ten years. Either we do it or they crush us.'
(Stalin, 1931)

Collectivization

Stalin also needed to increase the USSR's grain production. So, in 1929, he introduced collectivization to agriculture. Individual farms were merged into giant collectives (kolkhoz), which owned everything in common. Fierce resistance from property-owning peasants led Stalin to order the elimination of the kulaks (the wealthiest class). Ten million were shot, deported, or sent to labour camps. All this disruption led to a terrible famine (1932-33) in which six million peasants starved. Yet millions of tonnes of grain continued to be exported to subsidize the industrialization programme. Overall, collectivization was a huge disaster, from which agricultural production took a long time to recover.

The cost of collectivization

'A ruthless struggle is going on between the peasantry and our regime ... It's a struggle to the death ... It took a famine to show them who is master here. It has cost millions of lives, but the collective farm system is here to stay. We've won the war.'
(Communist Party official, 1932)

Women about to leave for work on the fields, on a collective farm in the Moscow region.

The great terror

In 1935, the assassination of Stalin's right-hand man triggered a series of purges against leading party members, as Stalin set about consolidating his power into a one-man dictatorship. His paranoia led him to include the military, intellectuals, party officials, peasants and workers among over 20 million victims, many of whom died in labour camps. The main conspirators were accused of plotting with the exiled Trotsky to overthrow Stalin. They were forced to denounce themselves in a series of public show trials (1936–38).

The Second World War

In 1941, Hitler invaded Russia in Operation Barbarossa. The Red Army was caught unprepared and forced to retreat. Eventual victory at the Battle of Stalingrad (1943) reinvigorated the Red Army, who pursued the retreating Germans all the way to Berlin. After the war, the continuing communist occupation of eastern Europe helped start the Cold War.

The Comintern (Third International)

In 1919, the Communist Party set up the Comintern (or Third International) to co-ordinate the activities of the international communist movement. The next year, delegates from 37 countries attended its second conference in Moscow and Lenin laid down strict conditions for admission to the association (the Twenty-One Points). This fatally undermined the European left-wing movement, by dividing it into competing camps (social democrats versus communists) and so preventing the emergence of any strong socialist parties during the turbulent inter-war period.

At first the purpose of the Comintern was to ensure Russia's survival, but when international socialism failed to materialize, it became an important tool of foreign policy. For example, during the Spanish Civil War (1936-39), Stalin used the Comintern to purge the revolutionary left from the Spanish Communist Party, in an attempt to curry favour with the Allies and so build an alliance against the rising threat of Germany

The Chinese Revolution

The founding of the Chinese Communist Party

On 4 May 1919, thousands of students in Beijing marched to Tiananmen Square, protesting against provisions in the Versailles Treaty which supported foreign interference in China's affairs. Their demonstration drew nationwide support and was a defining moment in Chinese politics. Inspired by the Russian example, radicals in the 4 May Movement went on to found the Chinese Communist Party (CCP) in Shanghai in 1921.

The Comintern persuaded the CCP to collaborate with the ruling Nationalist Guomingdang party (GMD), led by Dr Sun Yatsen. However, in 1925, relations between the two parties soured, after Chiang Kaishek became the new GMD leader. He had little sympathy with the communists, valuing the USSR's aid more than its ideology. In 1927, fearing their growing influence, Chiang ordered the slaughter of thousands of communists in Shanghai and other major cities.

Civil war

Over the next ten years, Chiang attempted to rule a disunited China, torn apart by competing local warlords. Harsh rule and widespread corruption lost him much popular support. Against Soviet advice, the communists abandoned the cities for the countryside, where their moderate land reforms and respect for the locals won them growing peasant support. Here they conducted a successful guerrilla campaign against superior GMD forces, setting up a communist mini-state in Jiangxi in 1931.

Fishes in the sea

Mao described the effectiveness of local support for the communists' guerrilla tactics:

'The people are the sea; and the army are the fishes swimming in the sea.'

The Long March, 1934–35

In 1934, the communists were forced to break out of their Jiangxi stronghold after a three-year siege. Harassed by GMD and warlord armies, the 90,000-strong communist Red Army marched over 10,000 km (6,000 miles) across mountain ranges and rivers. Only 7,000 made it to their new base in Shaanxi a year later. The heroic endurance of the Long March became an inspirational myth of the CCP. Its survivors went on to dominate the CCP until the 1990s. They included Mao Zedong, who became the party's new leader.

'Sailing the seas depends on the helmsman. Making revolution depends on Mao Zedong's thought,' was the caption to this 1969 poster.

Mao Zedong (1893-1976)

Mao Zedong (also Tse Tung) was China's first communist leader. He adapted communism to Chinese conditions by stressing the need for a rural rather than an urban-based revolution, and emphasizing agricultural development. His *Little Red Book of Quotations* was widely studied, earning him the nickname 'The Great Teacher'.

The son of wealthy peasants, Mao was one of the founders of the Chinese Communist Party (CCP). He established the People's Republic of China (PRC) in 1949, after a long civil war. In power, he was responsible for major agricultural and industrial developments, alongside the Sino-Soviet split, the chaos of the Cultural Revolution, and the deaths of millions of people through famine.

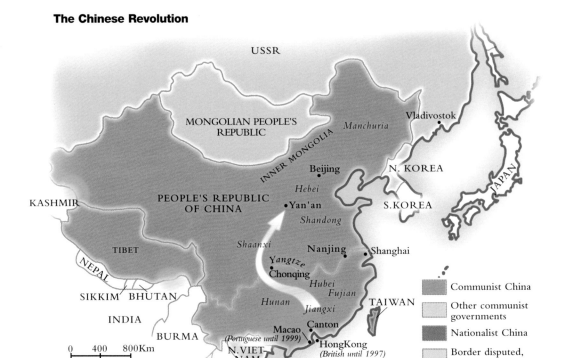

Legend:
- Communist China
- Other communist governments
- Nationalist China
- Border disputed, China and India
- The Long March

War with Japan and the founding of the People's Republic of China

In 1937, the Japanese launched a full-scale invasion of China and quickly overran its eastern seaboard. While the GMD retreated, the communists waged a successful guerrilla campaign in the north, which won them more popular support.

After the Japanese surrender in 1945, civil war soon resumed in China. The communists formed the People's Liberation Army (PLA), with captured Japanese weapons, and gradually broke down the GMD forces. By 1949, the PLA controlled the mainland and Chiang fled to Taiwan where he set up an alternative Chinese Republic with US backing. On 1 October, Mao proclaimed the People's Republic of China (PRC).

Mao faced the daunting task of modernizing a vast country, populated mainly by peasants, which had been torn apart by almost 40 years of civil war. Central planning, nationalization, price controls, and equality

In 1950, the year after it became a communist country, China invaded Tibet. In 1975, Laos also became a communist republic.

An inevitable truth

'Every Communist must grasp the truth, "Political power grows out of the barrel of a gun".'
(Mao, 1938)

Intervention in Korea, 1950-51

After the Second World War, Korea was divided into a communist-led North and a US-supported South. In 1950, the North invaded the South, but was pushed back across the 38th Parallel (Korea's internal border) by a United Nations (UN) peace-keeping force. When the UN invaded North Korea, Chinese troops intervened, forcing them to retreat. A cease-fire in 1953 returned Korea to its original division. Despite heavy casualties, China was pleased with its military success. But there were international repercussions. The USA gave massive aid to Taiwan, and allowed it to keep China's seat in the UN Security Council up until 1971.

for women were introduced to repair the shattered economy. Land reform was accompanied by thought reform, as Mao introduced the peasants to Marxist ideology via a massive propaganda campaign. Opponents were sent to labour camps for 're-education'.

In 1950, China signed an important friendship treaty with the USSR. Stalin provided substantial economic aid, including entire industrial plants and the scientists and technicians to run them. In 1953, the PRC adopted a Soviet-style Five-year Plan to develop its heavy industry.

A Hundred Flowers, 1956–57

By 1956, Mao was becoming frustrated at China's growing bureaucracy (encouraged by Soviet advisers). He called on Chinese intellectuals to 'let a hundred flowers bloom and a hundred schools [of thought] contend', hoping that they would offer constructive criticism of the situation. Instead he unleashed a torrent of abuse against the party and its rulers. In the backlash that followed, half a million of China's brightest thinkers were killed or imprisoned. Criticizing the communist foundations of China would not be tolerated.

This photograph was taken after Mao Zedong and other members of the Central Committee of the CCP had worked for a while alongside ordinary labourers constructing a reservoir near Beijing.

31

The Great Leap Forward, 1958–61

Despite its success, Mao was unhappy with the bias of the first Five-year Plan towards urban development. In 1958, he launched the 'Great Leap Forward' to strengthen the hold of communism in the countryside. Villages were merged into vast self-governing communes (averaging 30,000 peasants), in which agriculture and small-scale industry were combined to promote rural self-sufficiency. But it soon went horribly wrong. Officials were more interested in meeting their steel quotas (set by the party) than in harvesting their crops, and grain production fell drastically. Over 20 million died in the famine that followed. Before this utopian experiment, Mao had been revered by many as a national saviour. But its drastic failure reduced his influence in the party and a successful recovery programme was begun under Liu Shaoqi and Deng Xiaoping.

During the Great Leap Forward, photographs showed commune members enjoying great improvements in agricultural production.

The Sino-Soviet split

During the 1950s, Cold War propaganda portrayed a monolithic communist bloc led by Moscow. But cracks were beginning to show between China and the USSR. China disagreed with the USSR over ideology. It was angry when the new Soviet leader Khrushchev (Stalin's eventual successor) denounced Stalin's reign of terror and its crimes, at the Twentieth Party Congress in 1956. The shockwaves this caused rippled across the communist world. The Chinese communists, who had built their own rigidly authoritarian regime, were deeply offended and China began to reject the USSR's leadership of communism. Furthermore, Khrushchev's policy of 'peaceful coexistence' with the West appeared to abandon the communist doctrine of world revolution. In addition, China was upset at not being allowed to share the USSR's nuclear technology. Fed up with these criticisms, Khrushchev withdrew all Soviet aid to China in 1960. In 1962, relations worsened further when the USSR refused to back China over border conflicts with India.

A quotation of Chairman Mao

'Politics is war without bloodshed, while war is politics with bloodshed.'

The Cultural Revolution, 1966–69

In 1966, Chairman Mao launched the Cultural Revolution to regain control of the party. He was supported by Lin Biao, the PLA leader, who fuelled a growing personality cult by distributing millions of copies of Mao's *Little Red Book of Quotations* throughout China.

Red Guard slogans

'Mao Zedong is the red sun in our hearts.'

'Father is dear, mother is dear, but Chairman Mao is the dearest of all.'

Top: Red Army guards with *The Little Red Book*. **Above: a model from a revolutionary exhibition of a capitalist forced to read Mao's works.**

Under the slogan, 'Smash the old and bring in the new!', students known as Red Guards were encouraged to attack their teachers and anything associated with the past. Schools, factories and government institutions were closed down. 'Rightists', including Liu and Deng, were purged from the government, and thousands of people labelled 'counter-revolutionaries' were attacked, imprisoned, or killed. By 1968, China was on the verge of civil war. When the Red Guards turned on each other, the army was sent in to break them up. During the chaos of this period, a million people died and most economic production ground to a halt.

Mao tried to restore order. By 1975, he had rehabilitated Deng, established relations with the USA, and approved a new economic plan, known as the 'Four Modernizations' (agriculture, industry, the armed forces, and science and technology). His death in 1976 unleashed a violent power struggle between the Maoists and the moderates, which the moderates won.

Deng Xiaoping on his ninetieth birthday.

Deng Xiaoping (1904-97)

Deng Xiaoping succeeded Mao as China's leader. He was a landowner's son and studied abroad before joining the CCP. A Long March survivor, he was made General Secretary of the CCP in 1955, where his liberal ('rightist') views over the direction of China's economic development clashed with Mao's. He was ousted during the Cultural Revolution and then reinstated.

By 1978, he was in control of the party, promoting his reforms as 'socialism with Chinese characteristics'. His pragmatic rule restored domestic stability and economic growth, but his international reputation was tarnished by the Tiananmen Square massacre of 1989.

Students demonstrating for democracy, in Tiananmen Square, Beijing, in 1989. On this occasion, Deng Xiaoping's response to the demands of the protesters was to declare martial law. Chinese troops were brought in from the provinces to crush the pro-democracy movement. (See also page 57.)

'Socialism with Chinese characteristics'

By 1978, Deng had gained control of the CCP and began to reverse many of Mao's policies. China's development could not keep up with its rapidly growing population (which had doubled to a billion). Deng's solution was typically pragmatic: he introduced a one-child birth control programme (to lower population growth) and some free market reforms (to increase productivity). Farmers were allowed to sell their surplus at market prices (encouraging them to buy more as they became richer); private ownership was restored; and, most importantly, China's coastal zones were opened up to trade and foreign investment, importing valuable modern technology.

The results were dramatic. Led by booming rural industries, productivity and living standards shot up. China's annual GDP increased at an average rate of 10 per cent (triple that of the USA). But Deng's reforms brought unwelcome side-effects: unemployment, massive rural migration into the cities, increased corruption, and a widening social and economic gap between workers and the growing middle class. They also triggered demands for democratic reform, provoking large demonstrations in 1978, 1986 and 1989.

Cold War

After the Second World War, the USA and the USSR emerged as global superpowers. The 'Cold War' that developed between them was a conflict between two opposed political and economic systems, capitalism and communism. The capitalist West, led by the USA, saw itself as the champion of liberal democracy and a free market economy. It was determined to block the spread of the communist East. Each side thought its system was best, and tried to convince the world with the 'cold' weapons of propaganda, economics and technology. Both sides amassed large nuclear arsenals and used fierce words against each other. However, fear of nuclear annihilation ensured that they stopped short of real ('hot') war.

Communism in western Europe

During the economic chaos after the war, communism found strong support in France and Italy. By 1947, the Italian communist party (PCI) had two million members, making it the largest in western Europe. Appalled by the prospect of the PCI winning the 1948 elections, the US Central Intelligence Agency (CIA) sponsored a huge anti-communist propaganda campaign in Italy, involving the Catholic Church, to scare off the voters. It was the first of many such covert operations against the 'communist threat'.

In 1958, the Italian Christian Democratic Party issued this poster, warning people not to vote for the Italian communist parties. It depicts slave labour in the USSR.

A Revolution Day parade in Moscow.

An Iron Curtain

At the Yalta Conference in the Crimea in February 1945, the leaders of Britain, the USA and the USSR (Churchill, Roosevelt and Stalin), had agreed how they would carve up Europe once Germany was defeated. But afterwards, instead of keeping the promise he had made at Yalta to hold elections in eastern Europe, Stalin installed obedient communist regimes there, in order to create a protective buffer zone along the USSR's western border. It had been invaded three times in 150 years and Stalin wanted to ensure that this never happened again.

NATO and the Warsaw Pact

In 1949, the North Atlantic Treaty Organization (NATO) was set up to coordinate the defence of Western Europe and North America. The Warsaw Pact, formed in 1955, bound all the eastern bloc countries (except Yugoslavia) into an opposing alliance. Soviet troops were stationed across eastern Europe. When the Warsaw Pact disbanded in 1991, most of its members joined the North Atlantic Cooperation Council (part of NATO).

Truman's case

In 1947, President Truman explained why the USA should give financial support to Greece and Turkey in the fight against spreading communism:

'... the seeds of totalitarian regimes are nurtured by misery and want. They spread and grow in the evil soil of poverty and strife. They reach their full growth when the hope of a people for a better life has died. We must keep that hope alive .'

The USA misunderstood Soviet intentions, thinking the USSR's domination of eastern Europe was based on a policy of expansion rather than security. US President Harry Truman took a tough line. In 1947 the Truman Doctrine (which influenced US foreign policy until the Vietnam War) pledged the USA to contain the spread of communism throughout the world. Growing tension between the superpowers was aggravated by the USA's $13 billion Marshall Plan to redevelop western Europe, encouraging its war-ravaged economies to turn away from communism.

On a visit to the Berlin Wall in June 1963, US President John F. Kennedy spoke these now-famous words: 'All free men ... are citizens of Berlin, and therefore, as a free man, I take pride in the words *Ich bin ein Berliner.***'**

The Berlin blockade and airlift, 1948–49

After the war, Germany and its capital, Berlin, were divided in two. Soon the growing prosperity of the western zone (controlled by the USA, Britain and France) contrasted starkly with the poverty of the Soviet eastern zone. In 1948, the USSR closed all road and rail links between West and East Germany, isolating Berlin, which lay in the East. The Western Allies refused to abandon their zones of the city and defied the blockade by flying in two million tonnes of supplies over the next 10 months. Finally the USSR gave up and lifted the blockade. From then on, Berlin became a potent symbol – 'an island of freedom in the communist sea'. In 1961, the East German communists erected the Berlin Wall, to block off the main escape route. Hundreds of thousands of refugees had escaped to the west since 1945.

'Red Menace'

According to J. Edgar Hoover, leader of the Federal Bureau of Investigation (FBI) in the USA, communism was 'an evil way of life ... that spreads like an epidemic'. From 1946 the FBI ran a propaganda campaign across the media, against the 'Red Menace'. It even funded a movie, *The Street with No Name*. Later, Hollywood produced over 50 of its own 'Red Menace' movies.

In 1950, a right-wing senator, Joseph McCarthy, gained notoriety when he claimed there were over 200 communists inside the State Department. He made further unsubstantiated claims of communist infiltration inside Hollywood, the universities and even the United Nations, triggering a wave of anti-communist hysteria. The phrase 'reds under the beds' was coined, suggesting that communist sympathizers were to be found in the most unlikely places. Described by President Truman as a 'pathological character assassin', McCarthy went too far when he publicly accused the army and was sacked from his post by the Senate.

Rebellion in the eastern bloc

Stalin's death in 1953 brought a relaxation of the strict Soviet regime, raising hopes of liberalization among some satellite states. In 1956, Stalin's successor, Nikita Khrushchev, explained the new mood in a speech criticizing Stalin and arguing for 'peaceful co-existence' with the West. The same year, in Hungary, popular anger at the removal of the moderate leader, Imre Nagy, exploded in mass demonstrations. Nagy was re-instated, but his proposals for elections and withdrawal from the Warsaw Pact were too much for Khrushchev. The Soviet army was sent into Budapest, restoring order only after fierce fighting had left 2,000 dead.

Soviet tanks and some 200,000 troops moved in to Hungary, to put an end to the uprising in 1956.

Yugoslavia: a communist state apart

In Yugoslavia, the Communist Party came to power after the Second World War without Soviet help. Its charismatic leader, Marshall Tito, was too independent-minded for Stalin, refusing to take orders from Moscow. In 1948, Yugoslavia was expelled from the Soviet alliance and subjected to an economic blockade. Tito refused to give in, and Yugoslavia became the only independent communist state in Europe.

In 1968, a new regime in Czechoslovakia, under Alexander Dubcek, tried to make communist society more tolerant by proposing a series of reforms known as the 'Prague Spring'. Again, the USSR (now under the leadership of Leonid Brezhnev) came in to stamp out change and 'restore' order. Wherever communist rule was seen to be threatened, the Soviets intervened.

The Soviet economy

Khrushchev had promised to raise the Soviet standard of living to western standards, but this promise soon rang hollow after the initial successes of the space programme. While centralized economic planning brought full employment and fixed prices, it also encouraged waste and inefficiency. All jobs were

The Space Race

In 1961, Khrushchev proudly announced that communism would bury capitalism. The USSR had just launched the world's first satellite (Sputnik) and man (Yuri Gagarin) into space. Even space was not safe from the Cold War struggle, as the superpowers showed off their economic muscle-power.

The USA, having started badly, was determined to beat the USSR to the moon. While the Soviets made the first unmanned moon-landing, the Americans made the vital breakthrough in 1969, with the Apollo 11 mission. When pictures of Apollo 11 astronaut Neil Armstrong on the moon were broadcast around the world, the USA showed it was still one step ahead of its rival.

guaranteed for life, so there was no incentive for workers to increase their productivity. There was nothing to buy either, as luxury consumer goods were reserved for party members only. Queuing for essential items became a regular feature of daily Soviet life.

Demonstrators in Paris, May 1968.

Ernesto Che Guevara (1928-67)

'Che' Guevara was a professional guerrilla fighter, who became a symbol of revolutionary idealism after his death.

Born in Argentina, he became a Marxist after travelling across Latin America in the early 1950s. In Guatemala, he witnessed the US-backed overthrow of Arbenz's socialist regime, before joining up with Cuban revolutionary leader Fidel Castro in Mexico. He played an important role in the Cuban revolution (1956-59), and was a prominent member of Cuba's new communist government. In 1965, he left Cuba to resume his life as a guerrilla. He was captured and killed in Bolivia after trying to foment peasant revolution.

Rebellion in the West

In 1968, Marxist ideas helped inspire the student rebellions which swept across the USA and Europe. The May 'événements' in Paris came the closest to toppling a Western government. Demonstrations for university reform snowballed into part of a broader movement against the forces of capitalism and authoritarian government in general. Violent clashes with the police led to a huge popular demonstration against President de Gaulle's rule, and then to the biggest strike in French history, involving 10 million workers. But the movement was too divided to seize the moment and fizzled out.

Marxist terrorism

From the late 1960s, a new type of Marxist organization emerged in the West, using terrorism to destabilize the capitalist system. Groups such as the Red Army (Japan), Action Directe (France), the Red Brigades (Italy), the Red Army Faction or Baader-Meinhof gang (West Germany), and the Weathermen (USA) used bombing, kidnapping and assassination to attract attention to their revolutionary demands. Most of their targets were military, political or economic. Despite extensive media coverage, their activities achieved very little.

Mao's changing relations (from top): at Stalin's 50th birthday celebrations, 1950; with Khrushchev, 1957; and with President Richard Nixon, 1972.

Détente, 1969–75

During the 1970s, the Cold War entered a new period of détente, prompted by China's emergence onto the world scene. Each power had its own reasons for improving relations. The USSR wanted to reduce its defence spending, the USA wanted to end the Vietnam War, and China wanted to end its isolation.

Relations between China and the USSR had been in decline since the mid-1950s, and reached their lowest point in 1969, after border clashes brought them close to war. US President Richard Nixon exploited this division between the two communist powers, by opening up diplomatic channels with China (closed off after China's intervention in the Korean War) and then playing China off against the USSR. He hoped to lessen Soviet power and end the war in Vietnam, since the USA was convinced that China was backing North Vietnam.

In 1971, the USA ended China's international isolation by lifting its trade embargo and sponsoring China's entry into the United Nations (UN), in place of Taiwan. This was followed by an historic visit by President Nixon to Beijing in 1972. Fearing that an anti-Soviet coalition was being created, the USSR invited Nixon to the Kremlin and speedily signed the SALT disarmament treaty. China and the USSR were now competing for influence with the USA. It was a triumph of triangular diplomacy. For the USA, détente was a better way than aggression for managing its opponents.

The early 1970s also saw dramatic change in Europe. Willy Brandt, the West German Chancellor from 1969, pursued a new policy of cooperation with the East, known as Ostpolitik. In 1972, East and West Germany signed a treaty of mutual recognition, paving the way for the Helsinki Accords in 1975, in which NATO formally recognized all post-Second World War frontiers. In return, the communist bloc agreed to respect human rights. A spirit of cooperation was replacing decades of confrontation.

The end of détente, 1976–85

The late 1970s and early 1980s saw renewed tension. The Soviet deployment of more sophisticated missiles in Europe, the invasion of Afghanistan in 1979, and the shooting down of a Korean passenger plane in 1983, all contributed to growing distrust of the USSR and fuelled another arms race. Superpower relations only improved with the arrival of a new, reforming Soviet leader, Mikhail Gorbachev.

The spread of communism outside Europe

After 1945, communism spread rapidly beyond Europe. Even before China fell to Mao's communist army in 1949, Korea became 'infected' when it was occupied by the Soviets after the war. Communist regimes were soon established in Asia (Vietnam, Laos, Cambodia), South America (Cuba, Chile, Nicaragua) and Africa (Ethiopia, Mozambique, Angola).

West German Chancellor Willy Brandt (right) with the Soviet Prime Minister Alexei Kosygin at the signing of a treaty of friendship between their countries, in 1970.

43

Vietnam

Drawing inspiration from Mao's success in China, the Vietnamese communist leader Ho Chi Minh had to defeat both France and the USA before his country was finally reunited in 1976. From 1960, believing that South Vietnam needed to be defended against communism at all costs, the USA sent in troops to help defeat the communist rebels (Vietcong), who were trying to bring down the southern government and create a united Vietnam. However, mounting casualties and opposition to the war at home eventually forced the USA to withdraw its forces and sue for peace. Defeat in Vietnam was a humiliating blow for US prestige. It showed that a small determined country could defeat a heavily armed superpower.

Ho Chi Minh addresses villagers in North Vietnam, 1968.

Ho Chi Minh (1890-1969)

One of the century's most influential communist leaders, Ho Chi Minh was president of North Vietnam from 1954 to 1969.

After training in Moscow, he became the Asian representative to the Comintern during the 1930s. In 1941, he founded the Vietminh (League for the Independence of Vietnam) and led their struggle against the French (1946-54). Helped by his brilliant general, Vo Nguyen Giap, Ho's success relied on guerrilla tactics and the support of the peasantry. Despite victory, Vietnam remained divided. For the next 15 years, Ho led the struggle for reunification, in which the US-supported South was eventually outfought. After Ho's death, South Vietnam's capital (Saigon) was renamed in his honour – Ho Chi Minh City.

Cambodia

The Cambodian regime led by Pol Pot (1975-79) achieved international notoriety for its extreme version of communism. A disciple of Maoist 'total revolution', Pol tried to start a new society from scratch. All intellectuals were killed and whole cities were evacuated into vast countryside communes to work the land. During a three-year reign of terror, Pol's army, the Khmer Rouge, killed over a million people, a fifth of Cambodia's population.

Cuba

In 1959 the focus of East-West relations switched to Cuba after Fidel Castro and his guerrillas overthrew the discredited dictator, Fulgencio Batista. Castro's popular programme of land reforms and nationalization made him a hero in Cuba, but an enemy to the USA. By isolating Cuba with a trade embargo, the USA forced Castro into total dependence on Soviet aid. In 1961, Castro declared Cuba a communist state and went on to lend his troops to revolutionary movements in Angola, Ethiopia and Nicaragua.

Chile

In 1970, Dr Salvador Allende became the first democratically elected Marxist leader in the world. Convinced that Allende's government threatened US security and business interests, the CIA spent millions of dollars undermining his election and regime. Allende believed that communism could succeed without using violence. But his ambitious programme of social reform came to a violent end in 1973, when he was overthrown by a CIA-backed military coup. The repression that followed marked the end of the longest tradition of democracy in South America.

Instructions for CIA

Richard Helms, director of the CIA, noted down the instructions he received at a meeting with President Nixon just after Allende had won the presidential election:

'One in ten chance perhaps, but save Chile! ... not concerned risks involved ... no involvement of embassy ... $10,000,000 available ... full-time job – best men we have ... make the economy scream.'

The Cuban missile crisis, 1962

The Cuban missile crisis brought the USA and the USSR closer to war than any other incident and marked a turning-point in East-West relations. It began when a US spy-plane discovered Soviet-installed nuclear missiles in Cuba, within firing range of most US cities. President Kennedy demanded their removal and authorised a naval blockade to stop Soviet ships reaching Cuba. Khrushchev refused to budge and the two powers appeared on the brink of nuclear war. The showdown was resolved only after a face-saving compromise: the Soviet missiles were withdrawn in return for a US pledge not to invade Cuba and, in a secret deal, to withdraw NATO missiles from Turkey.

The nuclear threat

The fear that surrounded the Cold War came very much from its association with the development of nuclear weapons. To contain the nuclear threat, during the 1950s, US policy-makers worked out a deterrence theory based on mutual assured destruction (MAD). It was assumed that massive nuclear arsenals would prevent war, for no country would make a nuclear strike against an opponent known to have the capability of doing 'unacceptable damage' (destroying at least 25 per cent of the population and 50 per cent of industry) in retaliation. To keep the balance of terror, each side spent vast amounts on developing new technology, in order to keep up with its opponent.

In the USA, public spending on armaments benefited many companies, so that a powerful military–industrial complex was created against which no public figures dared speak out. In the USSR, a dual economy arose, as military investment constantly grew while the old agricultural-industrial economy was left to stagnate. The SALT treaty of 1972 marked an era of détente. But, by 1985, the USSR was nearly bankrupt after another arms build-up. The new Soviet leader, Mikhail Gorbachev, proposed a series of Strategic Arms Reduction Talks (START), which led to major reductions in all types of nuclear weapon.

Film fears

Dr Strangelove was a black-comedy film in 1963, which captured the nuclear jitters of the time. In it, a US airforce general says:

'I don't say we won't get our hair mussed, but I do say no more than ten to twenty million people killed.'

The Fall of the Iron Curtain

Gorbachev's reforms

When Mikhail Gorbachev became leader of the Communist Party in 1985, he inherited an ailing economy and a large national debt. He knew that the USSR needed radical change to survive. The traditional top-down command economy of communism would have to be modified. To this end, he launched a programme of economic restructuring (*perestroika*), to introduce a market economy. But he was immediately obstructed on two basic levels.

First, markets and socialism were viewed as ideologically incompatible. Most citizens saw private enterprise as a subversive activity. All they wanted were low prices and job security – both of which were threatened by greater economic efficiency. Without raising basic prices to more realistic levels, there could be no move to a market economy.

Second, the reforms were not in the self-interest of the party bureaucracy, whose ability to allocate state resources provided much of their power and privileges. Communism had created its own ruling elite (the *nomenklatura*), whose power was based not on property (as in the capitalist model), but on status (their position within the party hierarchy). To get around this, Gorbachev was forced to introduce a programme of *glasnost* (openness), to expose the bureaucracy to public criticism. But by weakening their position, *glasnost* also

Perestroika

'... [the] essence of perestroika is for people to feel they are the country's master.'
(Gorbachev, 1986)

Mikhail Gorbachev (left) and Boris Yeltsin, President of the Russian Federation, 1991.

Cooperation

'It is only through extensive international cooperation that we will be able to solve our most acute domestic problems.'
(Gorbachev, 1990)

Mikhail S. Gorbachev (born 1931)

The son of Russian peasants, Mikhail Gorbachev rose rapidly through the Communist Party ranks to become the youngest member of the Politburo in 1980. Elected general secretary in 1985, and president in 1988, Gorbachev led a new generation of party technocrats who wanted to reform the economy. But his reforms (*perestroika* and *glasnost*) had a much greater political impact, unwittingly causing the break-up of the USSR and the end of the Communist Party. In 1990, Gorbachev was awarded the Nobel Peace Prize for his role in ending the Cold War.

undermined the party's ability to implement its own reforms. By the time the Communist Party had approved the reform programme, the means to enforce it had been swept away by other changes beyond Gorbachev's control. For *glasnost* also brought unforeseen political reforms, by encouraging the open expression of public opinion and the formation of non-communist organizations across the USSR.

Gorbachev soon became caught in the middle of a fierce ideological battle between progressives and hard-liners within the Communist Party, and he was forced to slow down his reforms. Domestic problems such as miners' strikes, lengthening bread queues, and protests against the ban on vodka sales lowered his standing with the Russian people. By 1991, *perestroika* was considered a failure. A popular joke from the time suggested two solutions: either the USSR managed to sort out its own problems or, more likely, a UFO from Mars would land in Moscow and put everything right!

Gorbachev's need to revive the economy also led to radical changes in foreign policy. By winding down the Cold War, he slashed the huge costs of the Soviet empire – nuclear arms, military spending, and subsidies to other communist states. By ending Soviet intervention abroad and tolerating greater human rights at home (releasing political dissidents like the nuclear scientist, Andrei Sakharov), Gorbachev soon won over a cautious West. In December 1987, he signed the historic Washington agreement with US President

Ronald Reagan, eliminating all medium-range nuclear missiles. In 1988, he began the withdrawal of Soviet troops from Afghanistan, and announced a unilateral reduction of Soviet forces in eastern Europe. Overall, Gorbachev's reputation was much better abroad than at home.

The rise to power of Boris Yeltsin

In 1989, continuing obstruction to his reforms from conservatives persuaded Gorbachev to create a new parliament with some elected representatives, including critics like Boris Yeltsin and Sakharov. It became a forum for unprecedented criticism and debate. Yeltsin was a keen reformer, whom Gorbachev had brought into the Soviet leadership in 1985 to shake up the Moscow party. Two years later he was sacked after publicly criticizing the pace of reforms and the privileges of the ruling elite. This outspoken attack marked out Yeltin's future role as the people's champion.

As the party stalled on Gorbachev's reforms (private enterprise still accounted for only 0.5 per cent of the USSR's GDP), Yeltsin advanced. By June 1991 he had become the first elected president of the newly formed Russian Federation. Ironically, it was Gorbachev's reforms that had paved the way for his own downfall. By the time the Communist Party agreed to the principle of price increases and private enterprise, in April 1991, it was far too late. And even Moscow (now controlled by Yeltsin's Russian republic) could ignore Gorbachev's decrees with impunity.

Soviet dissident Anatoly Shcharansky was freed in 1986, as part of an East-West prisoner exchange.

Moldovans at a rally after their parliament had declared its independence, August 1991.

The soviet nationalities question

Meanwhile, a major problem was brewing on the borders. The Soviet Union was one of the world's most diverse states, containing 15 republics and 140 different nationalities. Russia, the largest, was surrounded by the Baltic states, the Ukraine, Georgia, Moldova, Belarus, and the Central Asian Republics. The *glasnost*-inspired revival of national identity throughout the Union soon led many of the republics to demonstrate for greater independence.

In March 1990, Lithuania became the first to officially declare its independence and was immediately denounced by Moscow. But Gorbachev's reluctance to use military force only encouraged similar movements in the other republics. Faced with continuing unrest, he eventually allied himself with conservatives and ordered a crackdown. But it was too late.

The Union Treaty, the coup and the formation of the CIS

In 1991, Gorbachev changed tactics and agreed to a new 'Union Treaty', which transferred much of the central government's power to the republics. Communist hard-liners (including the KGB) were unhappy at this and staged a coup to reimpose Soviet authority. Gorbachev was placed under house arrest, and the plotters announced his resignation. But they made a fatal mistake in not cutting the telecommunications networks, or arresting Yeltsin. Yeltsin's defiant public broadcasts from outside the Russian parliament made him the focus of public opposition to the coup, which collapsed within 48 hours. Key military leaders sided with Yeltsin and Russian troops refused to fire on their own civilians. Three people died. A week later the Communist Party was dead.

Immediately after the coup, most of the republics declared their independence and the Communist Party was abolished. In December, the presidents of the Russian Federation, Ukraine and Belarus formally dissolved the USSR, replacing it with the Commonwealth of Independent States (CIS).

Recognizing the absurdity of his position as president of a non-existent state, Gorbachev resigned on 25 December 1991. While the economic failures of communism had fatally damaged the USSR, it was the unforeseen consequences of *glasnost* which released the political genie from the bottle and allowed the final overthrow of the Soviet system. The great revolutionary experiment was over.

The fall of communism in eastern Europe

Communist rule had seemed so secure for 70 years that the events of 1989 took everyone by surprise. Communist regimes across eastern Europe (Poland, Hungary, East Germany, Bulgaria, Czechoslovakia and Romania) collapsed one after the other like dominoes. Two factors helped this happen: Gorbachev's support for political reforms in Poland and Hungary, and his rejection of the Brezhnev doctrine – the policy of Soviet military intervention to restore communist rule. Communist subjects (especially the young) reacted to the fall of the Berlin Wall in the same way as the French had responded to the destruction of the Bastille. Once the tyrants had lost the power to oppress, the people were no longer afraid.

Solidarity

The end of communist rule in Poland began in 1980, after a summer of industrial disputes led to the creation of Solidarity, an independent trades union movement. Led by Lech Walesa (below), it quickly became a national platform for opposition to the communist regime, boasting 10 million members at its peak. The threat was temporarily crushed in December 1981, when General Jaruzelski, the communist leader, imposed martial law on the country. Solidarity was banned, but continued to operate underground, boosted by the (Polish) Pope's visit and the awarding of the Nobel Peace Prize to Walesa in 1983.

Their Way

'The Brezhnev doctrine is dead ... You know the Frank Sinatra song "My Way"? Hungary and Poland are doing it their way. We now have the Sinatra doctrine.'
(Gennadi Gerasimov, Soviet government spokesman, October 1989)

Poland was the first to go, after industrial unrest brought the government and opposition together in February 1989 for a series of 'round-table' talks. In elections in June, Solidarity won most of the seats not reserved for the Communist Party. Solidarity's success did much to inspire other popular movements in eastern Europe and the USSR.

Romania

By December 1989, Romania was the last major communist state left in eastern Europe. Its fall was fast and bloody. Crowds surged through the streets of Timisoara and Bucharest, violent clashes left many dead, and a brutal tyrant (Nicolae Ceausescu) was toppled from power, after the army had switched sides.

Romania, June 1990: miners move in to deal with student protesters at Bucharest University.

A group of ex-communists, called the National Salvation Front (NSF), won the May elections. But accusations of voter intimidation provoked a large anti-government demonstration, which was violently dispersed by thousands of 'vigilante' miners. Disillusion soon followed, as the people realized that, despite the revolution, the old regime was still in power, but now under new management.

The fall of the Berlin Wall, 1989

In East Germany, the crisis began with a mass exodus of people during the summer of 1989. Thousands of East Germans escaped to the West through Hungary's newly opened border with Austria, while others sought asylum in West German embassies in Prague, Czechoslovakia, and Warsaw, Poland. Attempts to close the escape route through Hungary brought mass demonstrations (over 300,000 people) onto the streets of Leipzig and other East German cities. Shouting 'We are the people,' they demanded political reform.

Unable to rely on Soviet troops, the hard-line East German leader, Erich Honecker, was forced to resign. His successor, Egon Krenz, declared that direct travel to the West, with official permission, would be allowed. This was mistaken for a decision to open the Berlin Wall and border guards were unable to control the flow of people (over two million) who poured over the wall on 9-10 November. As they celebrated their freedom with rejoicing West Berliners, a new chant of 'We are one people' echoed through the country. The opening of the Wall signalled the end of communist authority and free elections were held in March 1990.

In July 1990, the East German currency, the Ostmark was replaced with the West German Deutschmark and East Germans were allowed to change their Ostmarks for Deutschmarks on a one-to-one basis. This was a windfall for East Germans with savings, and many went on a shopping spree.

German reunification

The continuing exodus of East German refugees placed great strains on West Germany. So reunification was brought forward to October 1990. But this worried the other European countries, who feared that an enlarged Germany might affect post-war stability. However, these concerns were soon

dwarfed by more pressing problems as East German industries collapsed, unemployment rose (to over 4 million), and there was a resurgence of neo-Nazism, with racist attacks on foreign workers and asylum seekers. To stem the growing economic divisions, Kohl raised taxes, but this only made the 'Wessis' (West Germans) resentful at having to support the 'Ossis' (East Germans). The honeymoon was over.

Victory

'Democracy has won ... The free market has won.'
(Zbigniew Brzezinski, US national security adviser, 1990)

A Communist Future?

Capitalism, not democracy, was the real winner of 1989. As huge fortunes were made in the new Russia, old hardships (food shortages) were replaced by new ones (soaring prices). Western advisers flooded in to eastern Europe to oversee widespread privatization. This soon led to falling industrial production and rising unemployment.

Freed from their political shackles, the federal states of eastern Europe divided into their constituent parts. Czechoslovakia peacefully split in two, but the break-up of Tito's Yugoslavia triggered years of savage warfare. The former USSR (the largest multi-national state) narrowly escaped a similar fate, although there were ethnic conflicts in Moldova, Azerbaijan, Georgia, and Russia; and civil war in Tajikistan.

While East and West Germany were re-united, the USSR, Czechoslovakia and Yugoslavia divided into smaller states.

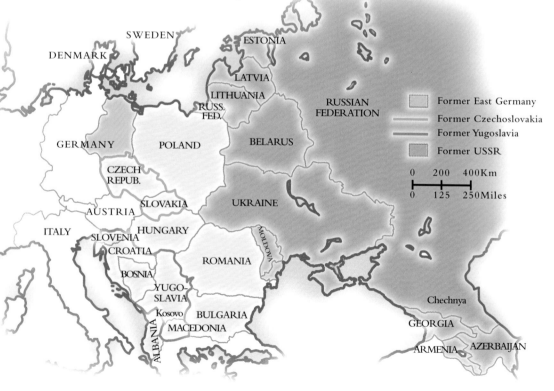

Former East Germany
Former Czechoslovakia
Former Yugoslavia
Former USSR

| 0 | 200 | 400Km |
| 0 | 125 | 250Miles |

SWEDEN
DENMARK
ESTONIA
LATVIA
LITHUANIA
RUSS. FED.
RUSSIAN FEDERATION
GERMANY
POLAND
BELARUS
CZECH REPUB.
SLOVAKIA
UKRAINE
AUSTRIA
ITALY
HUNGARY
SLOVENIA
MOLDOVA
CROATIA
ROMANIA
BOSNIA
YUGO-SLAVIA
Kosovo
BULGARIA
ALBANIA
MACEDONIA
Chechnya
GEORGIA
ARMENIA
AZERBAIJAN

The future of NATO

The security of a unified Europe depends on the relationship between NATO and Russia. The wish of all the ex-Warsaw Pact countries to join NATO left Russia feeling increasingly isolated. The 1997 NATO-Russia Founding Act went some way to easing these tensions, before the Czech Republic, Poland and Hungary joined NATO in 1999. Romania and Slovenia were due to follow.

Post-communist Russia

Russia experienced many difficulties during the transition from communism to a market economy. In 1993, President Yeltsin was challenged by a rebellious parliament and closed it down. After he had called in the army to restore order, he increased his presidential powers, so that he could fire and hire governments at will. In the subsequent elections, an extreme nationalist party and the re-formed Communist Party won the largest share of the vote. These results reflected growing opposition to the hardships of economic reform, the war in Chechnya, and the new mega–rich.

After Russia privatized the large state monopolies (like coal and gas), a small number of men became fabulously wealthy. Money equalled power in Yeltsin's Russia and a new financial oligarchy started to call the shots from behind the scenes. In 1998, 20 billion dollars of foreign aid were proved missing, believed to have been hidden abroad. Fingers pointed to an unholy alliance between the new political elites and the criminal 'maffiya'.

By the end of the 1990s, Yeltsin was a lame-duck president, sitting out his second term of office in between regular heart attacks and illness. Prime ministers and governments were dismissed on a regular basis. In 1999 Yeltsin resigned after recurring illness, having manoeuvred his chosen successor, Vladimir Putin, into position as the next president.

Few revolutions ever run smoothly. Whether Russia's second upheaval will continue peacefully towards a full free market remains to be seen. Continuing economic hardship could affect the future stability not just of Russia but of all the former Soviet republics. A demoralized army and the presence of nuclear weapons also pose a threat to future peace. In the post–communist world, the West cannot afford to ignore a weakened Russia.

Boris Yeltsin (born 1931)

Yeltsin was the first popularly elected leader in Russian history. He joined the Communist Party in 1961, and became Moscow Party Chief in 1985. His constant criticisms of the slow pace of President Gorbachev's reforms led to his sacking in 1987. But Yeltsin's popularity with the voters ensured a comeback in 1989, when he was elected first to the new Soviet parliament, and then President of the Russian Federation. His role in defeating the anti-Gorbachev coup in 1991 confirmed his growing power. In December 1991, he formally abolished the USSR and the Communist Party. As president, he pushed through an unpopular programme of economic reforms, survived a coup, and launched two military offensives against Chechnya. His private behaviour brought regular accusations of drunkenness and abuse of power. He resigned his position at the end of 1999.

A food queue in Moscow, December 1998.

East Germany

In Germany too, the Communist Party rose from the dead. Renamed the Party of Democratic Socialism (PDS), it polled 25 per cent of the vote in the 1999 eastern regional elections, and gained seats in the Bundestag and European parliament. Its success came from resentment at the widening social divisions between east and west after reunification. Supporters of the party claimed that, at least under communism, everyone was guaranteed work and cheap housing.

1998: a protest by unemployed East Germans, whose placards say they would take any job.

Pragmatic Deng

'To get rich is glorious' and 'It does not matter whether a cat is black or white as long as it catches mice.'

These aphorisms used by Deng Xiaoping sum up his pragmatic stance towards communism. The first became his slogan for a 1992 tour of the booming coastal cities.

China

In 1999, China celebrated its 50th anniversary as a communist state. Deng Xiaoping's 'socialism with Chinese characteristics' looked very different from Mao's version, but the two leaders shared a ruthlessness in dealing with any threats to their rule. In June 1989, Deng ordered a crackdown on the pro-democracy movement, and demonstrations for multi-party rule were met with tanks and guns. At least 1,000 students and workers were killed, while thousands more were imprisoned or fled the country.

Today's threat to the Chinese government comes from the Falun Gong, a growing spiritual movement with over 70 million members. After it was banned in July 1999, a well-organized campaign of peaceful protests, coordinated over the Internet, was followed by thousands of arrests. History shows why the Falun Gong is so feared, as mystical movements have often played a leading role in Chinese rebellions.

The dangers of economic reform

During the nineteenth century, China was the world's largest economy until it was overtaken by the USA. At the current rate of growth, it should regain its dominance by 2020. But the costs are high, with rising inflation and unemployment. In 1994, the brakes were applied: price controls were reintroduced on essential items (like food and rent), and reforms of the overmanned state-owned enterprises (SOEs) were postponed. SOEs account for half of China's total production, and rely on huge state subsidies. If the government slims them down, late 1990s unemployment levels of around 15 per cent (out of a population of 1.3 billion) will rise drastically, threatening China's social stability.

The rest of the world

Outside China, only a handful of communist regimes survive: Vietnam, North Korea and Cuba. All have struggled with their economies since the collapse of the USSR, and all share China's problem of pursuing economic reforms while preventing simultaneous political reforms which would threaten the monopoly of the Communist Party. These regimes have lasted because of their strong anti-colonial roots, and because they have adapted to local needs – self-reliance in the case of North Korea and national identity in Cuba.

Cuba illustrates well the problems of adapting to post-USSR life. During the 1990s, people predicted Cuba's imminent collapse as severe shortages and growing unrest threatened Castro's regime. Tourism and private investment eased the country's troubles, creating a dual economy (US dollars alongside Cuban pesos). But instead of raising living standards, the influx of dollars only increased social inequality. Fed up with the constant rhetoric of 'sacrifice', many Cubans (including Castro's own family) voted with their feet and chose to emigrate to the USA.

Cuban refugees at a detention centre in Miami, Florida, in the summer of 1994.

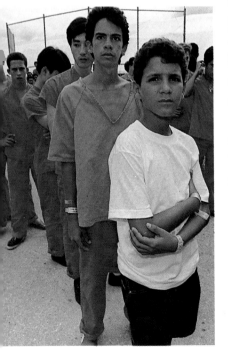

A new world order

Has the end of the Cold War created a safer or more dangerous world? Superpower predictability has been replaced by multi-power unpredictability. Conflict over scarce natural resources (such as oil or water), rather than ideology, poses the biggest threat to peace today. Powers will compete to satisfy the growing energy demands of their economies, and new global alliances will respond to an increasingly powerful China.

The end of communism?

So where does communism stand at the beginning of the new millennium? Marx described a socialist utopia where 'the free development of each [allows] the free development of all'. His big mistake was to believe that such a utopia could be realized in a society stripped of financial incentives. Even under Stalin, the Communist Party rewarded its leaders with perks such as cars and holiday dachas. The story of communism in the twentieth century showed the practical impossibility of building such utopias. No communist leader reached beyond the 'dictatorship of the proletariat' to the final stage of pure communism. Neither Lenin's NEP, nor Stalin's collectivization, nor Mao's Great Leap Forward could deliver on the promise of self-sufficiency for all.

However, we should not lose sight of Marx's major insight, that the key to a better life is less work and more play. He believed that, when people were freed from material struggle (with machines doing most of the work), human creativity would thrive on a diet of science, art, and community spirit. In this brave new world, life's simple pleasures, like eating a peach, or playing games, would be as important to human development as building a road or producing steel. If there is a future for communism and Marx's thought, it belongs to changing the way we think about the world and live our lives, rather than in grand schemes of forcing whole nations into a communist utopia.

The future

'I think that the future belongs to democracy but not to capitalism, because they are opposite camps. We believe the government has to intervene precisely for the benefit of those who would be deprived if you leave democracy to the market.'
(Ricardo Alarcon, president of Cuba's National Assembly of People Power, 1998)

Date List

1789	Fall of the Bastille and start of the French Revolution.
1818	Birth of Karl Marx.
1848	Publication of *The Communist Manifesto*. Revolutionary explosion across Europe (the 'Springtime of the Peoples').
1864	Marx helps to found First International.
1870	Birth of Lenin.
1871	Rise and fall of the Paris Commune.
1879	Birth of Stalin.
1890	Birth of Ho Chi Minh.
1893	Birth of Mao Zedong.
1898	Russia's first Marxist party founded by Georgy Plekhanov.
1903	Russian Social Democratic Workers' Party splits into Menshevik and Bolshevik factions.
1904	Birth of Deng Xiaoping.
1905	'Bloody Sunday' demonstration outside Winter Palace in St Petersburg leads to widescale rebellion; formation of first soviets.
1912	Russian Bolshevik Party founded.
1917	Revolution in Russia; Lenin becomes first communist leader. 4 May student protest movement in Beijing, China.
1914	Germany declares war on Russia.
1918	Brest-Litovsk treaty and execution of Tsar and family. Spartacist uprising in Germany; execution of Rosa Luxemburg.
1919	Formation of Third International (Comintern).
1919–20	The Russian Civil War.
1921	New Economic Policy.
1921	Kronstadt Rising. Chinese Communist Party founded.
1924	Death of Lenin.
1927	Chiang Kaishek becomes leader of the Guomindang.
1928	Birth of Che Guevara. Beginning of Stalin's first Five Year Plan.
1929	Stalin takes full control of the Soviet Communist Party.
1931	Birth of Mikhail Gorbachev.
1934–35	The Long March of the Chinese Communist Party (escaping from the GMD).
1935	Stalin's 'Great Terror' begins.
1936–39	Spanish Civil War.
1937	War begins between Japan and China.
1939–45	Second World War.
1945	First atomic bomb exploded over Japan by the USA. Vietminh proclaim independence of Vietnam.
1948	Marshall Plan starts to rebuild Europe's ravaged economy.
1948–49	Berlin blockade and airlift.
1949	Mao proclaims the People's Republic of China. Chiang Kaishek moves GMD to Taiwan and proclaims a separate Chinese Republic, taking China's seat in the UN. Formation of NATO.
1950–53	Korean War.

1954	Fall of Dien Bien Phu; French leave Vietnam.
1956	Soviet troops occupy Hungary.
1958	Mao launches the Great Leap Forward.
1959	Castro takes power in Cuba.
1960	USA intervenes in Vietnam.
1961	Construction of Berlin Wall begins.
1962	Cuban missile crisis.
1965	First anti-Vietnam War protest in Washington, DC.
1966	Mao launches the Great Socialist Cultural Revolution.
1967	Che Guevara captured in Bolivia and killed.
1968	Student protests sweep across Europe and the USA; rioting in Paris nearly brings down de Gaulle's government. Soviet troops occupy Czechoslovakia.
1969	USA lands first man on moon.
1970	Salvador Allende becomes world's first elected Marxist leader in Chile.
1972	Nixon arrives in China. SALT treaty signed.

1973	Ceasefire between North and South Vietnam. Allende's government overthrown in military coup.
1975	Fall of Saigon; communists gain Cambodia as well.
1976	Death of Mao Zedong.
1978	Deng Xiaoping takes power.
1979	Russian troops invade Afghanistan.
1980	Founding of Solidarity by Lech Walesa.
1985	Gorbachev becomes General Secretary of Soviet Communist Party.
1989	Pro-democracy demonstrations in Tiananmen Square are crushed by Chinese troops. Fall of Berlin Wall; peaceful collapse of Iron Curtain across Eastern Europe apart from Romania.
1990	Reunification of Germany.
1991	Boris Yeltsin elected President of the Russian Federation. Failed coup; dissolution of the USSR and the Soviet Communist Party; resignation of Gorbachev.
1999	Resignation of Yeltsin.

61

Glossary

bourgeoisie
the capitalist ruling class (in Marxist thought); otherwise the middle classes in general.

Brezhnev doctrine
the USSR's policy of intervening to protect communist governments in eastern Europe.

CIA (Central Intelligence Agency)
the US equivalent of the Russian KGB, created in 1947 to coordinate and run espionage and intelligence activities.

dacha
country house or cottage in Russia.

détente
the relaxation of tensions between nations.

dictatorship
the rule of a dictator, who is not bound by any laws or constitution.

feudalism
the legal and social system that evolved in Europe during the Middle Ages, in which peasants were protected and looked after by their lords in return for their service on the land and in war.

free market
economic system in which prices are allowed to go up and down according to supply and demand.

GDP (gross domestic product)
the value of domestic goods and services provided annually by a nation.

GNP (gross national product)
the total value of all goods and services provided annually by a nation.

guerrilla warfare
using irregular soldiers to harass the opposing army through acts of sabotage, ambush, etc.

KGB
The USSR's 'Committee for State Security', a secret police organization responsible for espionage and intelligence operations.

Maffiya
Russian variation on the Italian term (Mafia) for organized crime.

oligarchy
government by a small group of people.

Politburo
the chief policy-making body of the Russian Communist Party; succeeded by the Presidium of the Central Committee in 1952.

privatization
taking into private ownership a company that has previously been owned by the state.

proletariat
the industrial workers in a capitalist society, whose only real possession is their labour (in Marxist thought); otherwise the working classes in general.

SALT (Strategic Arms Limitation Talks)
the first major arms control treaty, signed by Presidents Nixon and Brezhnev in 1972.

socialism
idea that a country's wealth should be shared out more equally. Unlike communists, socialists accept democracy and changes of government by free elections.

totalitarian
relating to a dictatorial one-party state that regulates every area of life.

utopia
any real or imaginary society or place considered to be perfect (from the Greek meaning 'no place').

Resources

Reference

M. Almond, *Revolution – 500 Years of Struggle* (de Agostini, 1996) chronicles 25 of the world's greatest revolutions, using eyewitness accounts.

S. Crawshaw, *Goodbye to the USSR* (Bloomsbury, 1992) describes the final years of the Soviet Union, with many eyewitness accounts.

J. Isaacs and T. Downing, *Cold War* (Bantam Press, 1998) contains lots of photographs and interesting stories.

A. Mazower, *Dark Continent: Europe's Twentieth Century* (Penguin, 1999) offers a controversial view of how fragile Europe's democracy has been.

D. McLellan, *The Thought of Karl Marx* (Papermac, 1971) is widely regarded as the most comprehensive introduction in English.

J. Reed, *Ten Days that Shook the World* (Penguin, 1919) is a vivid eyewitness account of the October Revolution, by an American journalist.

Fiction

Dr Zhivago (1957), by Boris Pasternak, is set in the first ten years of the Russian Revolution. It was suppressed in Russia but acclaimed as an international masterpiece.

George Orwell's *Animal Farm* (1945) and *1984* (1949) are brilliant satires attacking the Soviet regime's hypocrisy and totalitarianism.

Arthur Miller's play *The Crucible* (1953) draws a disturbing parallel between the hysteria of the 17th-century witch trials in Salem, Oregon, and the communist witch-hunts of Senator McCarthy (see page 39).

One Day in the Life of Ivan Denisovich (1962) by Alexandr Solzhenitsyn is a fictional account of life in a gulag, drawn from personal experience.

Films

Dr Strangelove (1963), by Stanley Kubrick, is a satire on the mad logic which underpinned the nuclear arms race.

Francis Ford Coppola's *Apocalypse Now* (1979) is probably the best of a string of Vietnam movies from the late 1970s and early '80s.

Index